"Proud and Beautiful: Embracing Black Excellence"

€ 2024 by Selena L.L. Arnold All rights reserved.

Unauthorized use or reproduction of any portion of this book is strictly prohibited without the author's prior written consent, except for brief quotations allowed for book reviews.

ISBN/SKU: 979-8-8691-5221-3

"Believe you can and you're halfway there."

"The only way to do great work is to love what you do."

"Every moment is a fresh beginning."

"You are never too old to set another goal or to dream a new dream."

"Success is not final, failure is not fatal: It is the courage to continue that counts.

"The future belongs to those who believe in the beauty of their dreams."

"In the middle of difficulty lies opportunity."

"Don't watch the clock; do what it does. Keep going.

"Your time is limited, don't waste it living someone else's life."

"Strive not to be a success, but rather to be of value."

"It's not whether you get knocked down, it's whether you get up."

"The only limit to our realization of tomorrow will be our doubts of today."

"Success is stumbling from failure to failure with no loss of enthusiasm."

"The journey of a thousand miles begins with one step."

"Do not wait to strike till the iron is hot, but make it hot by striking."

"Don't be pushed around by the fears in your mind. Be led by the dreams in your heart."

"Believe in yourself and all that you are. Know that there is something inside you that is greater than any obstacle."

"The only way to achieve the impossible is to believe it is possible."

"Opportunities don't happen.
You create them."

"What lies behind us and what lies before us are tiny matters compared to what lies within us."

"Your attitude, not your aptitude, will determine your altitude."

"Don't count the days, make the days count."

"The only place where success comes before work is in the dictionary.

"Dream big and dare to fail."

"The best way to predict the future is to create it."

"Success is not in what you have, but who you are."

"Challenges are what make life interesting.
Overcoming them is what makes life meaningful."

"What you get by achieving your goals is not as important as what you become by achieving your goals."

"Your life does not get better by chance, it gets better by change."

www.ingramcontent.com/pod-product-compliance
Lightning Source LLC
LaVergne TN
LVHW062045070526
838201LV00081B/3069